To Amanda

10 Minutes a Day
with Coach Cath

Business Social Media

I hope you enjoy &
benefit from my 1st
Book!

Cath x

Dec
2020.

Endorsed by

"Social media is so important to build business today and to ensure you're visible. The 10 minutes a day, every day approach is a fantastic way to get into the habit of being consistent on social media. Thanks Cath!"

Marie Elizabeth Edwards

Founder: Made by Mee, Mee and You Networking

10 Minutes a Day with Coach Cath

Business Social Media

Cath Babbington

Publications

Contents

Foreword

I grew up a Grocer's daughter in a time long before social media! My early years were spent living above the shop - an Aladdin's cave, full of wondrous things: large glass Apothecary Jars filled with sweets and shoelaces; fresh food stacked high; and reliable hardware. All was infused with the delicious smells of home cooked hams and pies.

When we were forced to move, I still spent most holidays and Saturdays in the new shop. Pocket money was earned by cutting cheese into smaller amounts and wrapping it in wax paper, or sitting on an upturned bucket weighing out potatoes into small, brown, paper bags from huge sacks. Most often, it comprised of walking up and down all the surrounding roads and putting a leaflet through each door with that week's offers – marketing!

For me, marketing was just a way of life. I thought it all just good, common sense. Frankly, I couldn't understand all the fuss when marketing and business were spoken about as if it was a secret code.

In the early 90s, there was, what I will refer to as, 'The Cult of the MBA'. Clever people, with good first degrees, would learn all about business and marketing in a classroom then give lesser mortals, like me, advice. So much so, that while running my own million pound and hugely successful PR company, I even considered a part time MBA to add credibility to my offering. Thankfully, a good friend told me not to. He said, *"You know more about good business and real-life marketing than anyone I've met. Trust what you understand."*

He was right.

A customer at the time published an industry white paper that took the market by storm. It was called: *'It can't be bought if it isn't there.'* Genius, hey?!

Well, today you or your product or service can't be bought if no one sees it or you. Visibility is key - and visibility on social media is crucial.

Right from the start, this little, but powerful, book (brought to you by Coach Cath) offers practical advice and pitches you straight into exercises giving you workable solutions. It is the modern-day equivalent of pointing out: what you have to offer the world can't be bought if you are *'not there'*.

There is a great saying, *'Its not knowing what to do that is important, it is doing what you know'*. I think, *'True, but finding time to do what you know is often the challenge.'* So, when Cath's book instructs *'what and how to do social media'* in only 10 mins a day - you are onto a winner! Not only is Cath's brilliant book straightforward, she uses her personal experiences of tried and tested social media tools and platforms to guide you to success.

Being visible is often an action that people unconsciously hold back from. The mantras *'Children should be seen and not heard'* and *'Talking about yourself is vain'*, is engrained in the British psyche. This needs to change: this book gives you permission to tell your audience and customers about your wonderful product or service. It is not vanity but necessity. As an adult businessperson, you are allowed to share the news about your products and services.

You or your product can't be bought if it isn't there or in today's world seen to be there. Social media is the way to gain that visibility and free marketing.

Coach Cath can help you to be seen and get in front of the market that is right for you. This book is authoritative in its simplicity: Cath makes the process easy and fun. Ten minutes a day investment in time is a small price to pay to find the most brilliant you.

What are you waiting for?

Take your first 10 minutes and boost your business social media today.

It is your time to shine.

Rosalyn Palmer, September 2020.

Rosalyn is an award-winning Transformational Therapist and Coach. Bestselling Author of *Reset! A Blueprint for a Better Life* and co-author of three Amazon No.1 bestselling self-help books including *Ignite for Female Changemakers*.

*The secret to getting ahead
is getting started.*

Mark Twain

Welcome to the Social Media Jungle!

Hello and welcome. I'm so glad you have bought this book; we're going on an exciting Social Media adventure together.

My name is Cath, and my business is CoachCathUK. I'm a busy working mum. I'm a sole trader, and I'm grateful to be very good at what I do and to be successful. I work hard and am always looking for maximum returns from my social media with as little time as possible as I don't have much to spare – just like you. My years of being at the sharp end of Operational and Human Resource Management means I have practical experience in all types of business which I bring to this book and to you. I changed my career and went into training and teaching for many years following the birth of my son, then took the leap and became self-employed (over 13 years ago) – *and I have NEVER looked back.*

Social media is a business skill you need to learn – as someone born in the '70s, I'm what they call a *'Digital Immigrant'* (Prensky 2001) so I wasn't brought up with social media as younger generations have – *I remember my first mobile phone was like a brick!* and *'My Space'* along with *'Friends Reunited'* were all the rage when online connecting first started.

Years ago, marketing was out of reach for so many of us and involved branding, TV, press, and lots and lots of paid advertising. It was really expensive and often overwhelming for the average person. As a business skill, maximising your presence on social media is an AMAZING opportunity to market you and your business for free!

We now live in a society which is dominated by lots of different social media platforms and you can use this for free, at any time of the day or night, in any way to promote, share and make money from your business – *how fantastic is that?*

- ✋ FREE marketing

- ✋ ANY time to suit you

- ✋ ACCESSIBLE anywhere in the world

WOW!

Hang on, if it's this easy, and costs nothing at all – why do you need to buy this book?

Education costs money.
But then so does ignorance.

Sir Claus Moser

Sometimes, we all need help in business. I speak to many entrepreneurs, just like you, and so many of them struggle to understand that a social media platform is a business tool, and just like doing your tax return, needs to be a dedicated part of your business. You need to invest time and attention into your social media strategy, for your business to benefit from it. *Easier said than done, I know, hence why you're reading this now, I guess?*

I was inspired to write this book as a *'quick and easy'* solution to understanding and maximising the return on investment of your time on social media. It's about keeping things quick and simple. *Ten minutes a DAY is my target for you.* I'm not going to tell you how to write lots of original, lengthy, strategic copy – that's great when you have the time – but this is about a busy business owner who needs a social media presence on their chosen platform and needs it in the most easy and effective way possible.

This book teaches you a visible, and consistent strategy with a variety of content that gets you out there and drives your reach and engagement. It is laid out with information and detail from; how you can choose the right platform to *'match'* your business market and customers, to what the different platforms do, and how to use them.

There is a month by month *'evergreen'* calendar which gives you an activity to do every day and so takes the *'What the heck do I put online today?'* worry away totally. *Just follow the monthly plan and you'll be fine.*

In the planner, I offer you marketing suggestions for each month, with a 'heads up' on things you could do alongside the planner, to make your content more specific to your business. I also give you some great ideas for key events such as Christmas or Valentine's Day – even if your product or service doesn't have a direct link to these special events. Using them in your social media content will keep you up to date and relevant.

Social Media, like all things in life, involves practice. The idiom rings true *'practice makes perfect'*. A daily habit of using social media - or a weekly habit of scheduling your content (*YES, I cover that too!*) will bring you massive benefits – maybe not straight away, but over a reasonably short time.

You'll see people connecting with you, understanding you and your offer, engaging with your posts and then, buying from you... It's like the flywheel effect (Collins, 2001) the more you do something, the better it gets and the more energy it generates.

How does the flywheel effect work then?

The flywheel effect, in the image below, shows the social media 'public' – your existing customers, prospects, or potential customers, strangers, and promoters. These are people who love what you do. *I will go into more detail in Part 6: Marketing Basics.*

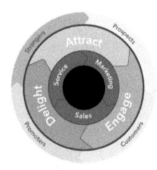

Your content should attract, delight, and engage with 'the public' on social media, to convert strangers to prospects and prospects to customers, and customers to promoters in this virtuous circle. *Are you with me so far?*

Then your content goes deeper and actively promotes your service or product, sells it, and markets its benefits. The centre or hub of the flywheel is your success. The trick is to maintain the momentum of the flywheel and keep it going. This is similar to something we often call a *'sales funnel'* and is the concept behind this book - to keep your social media content highly visible and helping convert strangers into customers! If you're struggling, think of it like a black hole at the centre and the gravitational pull slowly drawing your customers from the outer edges inwards!

Take a moment to reflect on this short introduction and what it means for your business success on social media. Make a note here on why you purchased this book and what you wanted to achieve from it to help you stay motivated as you continue this exciting new journey with me.

Coach Cath

Your Notes

I purchased this book because:

_____

_____

_____

I want to achieve:

_____

_____

_____

_____

True life is lived
when tiny changes occur.
Leo Tolstoy

Part 1
Creating a Habit

Success usually comes to those who are too busy to be looking for it.

Henry David Thoreau

Turn Up Every Day on Your Chosen Platform

I n the introduction, we looked at the flywheel effect, the work of guru Jim Collins. *I love his book, Good to Great, give it a try if books are your thing!!* Learn to generate this flywheel effect, *think like a black hole, remember?* You need to engage, attract and delight your audience on social media.

The key to doing this with social media in any business is to show up consistently.

Coach Cath's Top Tip
Just show up!

Any platform you choose, any product you sell, and any service you offer will only be purchased IF people know it's there. Visibility is the first step.

One of the issues with social media is that it is made up of *'scrollers'*. These are people who dip into and out of their phones for a few minutes here and there, trawling through 1000's of posts, images, and videos and dismissing them with a swish of the finger – gone!!

We have developed a short attention span, and this is an issue for anyone using social media for their business. I know a lot of experts are out there. Each has their methodology of how to be seen on social media. We often associate these with the term 'influencers' and they each have different ways of working with a chosen platform and have different terms for what they do. *I'll explain these in the next chapter to help with the confusion, so breathe, I'm here to help you succeed.* However they ALL have the same common principle: you need to have a constant meaningful presence on social media, over some time, to be noticed.

Content is important, which is where this book will help you so much, but if you are going to do this in 10 minutes a day, then it's about maximising your time and putting yourself out there, daily, regardless.

Your Notes

What stops me from investing 10 minutes a day in growing my business through social media?

_____

_____

_____

_____

The hardest thing is getting started; the second hardest thing is maintaining momentum!

Remember - any time and place, anywhere. You have to show up daily and let your audience know you are there and want to connect with them, nurture them, and do business with them.

"But Cath, I know this, but I still don't feel committed to spending this time every day."

I hear you... And yeah SO MANY small business owners really struggle with being accountable to themselves for this task as it genuinely is a 24/7 job. Often it doesn't see a quick return, so it feels like you're putting in a whole lot of effort for very little action.

Yes, at first it IS like that, but remember the flywheel effect? It takes time to start it going, regularity and consistency, and then in a few weeks and months you'll see a real difference – people will feel they know you and your business, they will know what you do. They will have built a relationship with you online and so will do business with you rather than someone else, your competitor, doing a similar thing (and there is ALWAYS someone else doing a similar thing).

A dream is just a dream.
A goal is a dream with a plan
and a deadline.

Harvey MacKay

Creating the Social Media Habit

I've heard it said that up to 40% of what we do every day is down to the habits we have made over our lifetime. An interesting viewpoint, but I do know introducing new habits, (like exercise) are really hard, and that breaking old habits, (such as smoking) can be incredibly difficult. So, I thought I'd add a section here to give you some ideas on how to start and maintain your new 10 minutes a day social media habit.

Making a new habit really easy and accessible is perhaps the best way to start. Let's apply this theory – making posting on social media an easy, small habit you'll make on a consistent basis.

Why would you say, "No?"

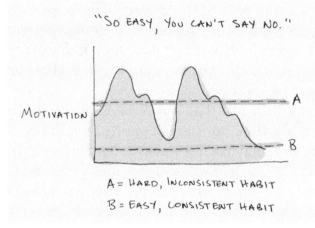

"SO EASY, YOU CAN'T SAY NO."

MOTIVATION

A

B

A = HARD, INCONSISTENT HABIT

B = EASY, CONSISTENT HABIT

Have a look at this graph by James Clear (from James Clear.com), it shows if you want to make a new habit – such as investing time for your business on social media – your motivation can go up and down. Sometimes, you are highly motivated to deliver your social media posts, others less so.

Therefore, if you want to make a new habit, it needs to be simple, consistent and easy to implement. Doing a little every day builds the habit *'muscle'* and gives you the win of small changes adding up over time.

I'm not asking you to create meaningful social media content involving lots of hard thinking or difficult subjects to cover. I'm saying you can achieve meaningful social media content with the business goals you want using the correct monthly planner as your daily guide. *Easy as that!*

Make it so easy you can't say no.

Leo Babauta

Goal setting is another useful business tool, ensuring you make a specific commitment, which is crystal clear. You may have heard of an acronym called SMART, which stands for Specific, Measurable, Achievable, Relevant, Time-bound.

Your SMART Goals

A SMART goal for posting on social media might be something like this?

> I commit to using the planner in this book, daily, before 10am, to post once on LinkedIn and connect with my ideal business customers for up to 10 minutes afterwards 7 days a week, starting today.

Can you see the difference using a SMART goal makes? It really 'nails' exactly what you are promising to do with no wiggle room at all. Maybe look at the commitment on the next page and make it a SMART style goal.

Lack of accountability is also an often-used excuse for not delivering on a habit. This might be why businesses such as *Slimming World* and *Weight Watchers* are so successful. Is it that we didn't know all the stuff they talk about? *Of course not!* It's the weekly weigh-in and accountability that these programmes offer its members which helps support them to take action.

Success is the sum of small efforts
– repeated day-in and day-out.

Robert Collier

Think about it. If this 10 minute a day social media activity was in a job description you had as an employee, and your boss was checking on you daily, you KNOW you'd find the time to get it done wouldn't you? So be accountable for your own behaviour and invest in your own business in exactly the same way you would in someone else's.

How can you hold yourself accountable?

Try this activity right now! Make a list of the benefits of social media marketing RIGHT NOW. *It's the last page of this chapter and is really important.*

Write it down, get it visible. Take a photo and post it on your social media to make the commitment public if you like, just embrace this change, and make it so. Put a note in your office, on the fridge, even on the toilet to remind you to and *'nag'* you to do this one, easy activity every day. Yes, the rewards are not instant but you've invested in this book, and want to improve your social media marketing, so your business will reap the benefits. Make the commitment and make it happen.

YOU HAVE GOT THIS!!!

Your Notes

My Business Benefits.

The benefits for my business by turning up every day on social media are:

_____

The barriers I struggle with:

_____

Why I want to do this now:

_____

This is how I will dedicate 10 minutes a day, every day to this business priority?

_____

My *'SMART'* Commitment is:

_____

Posted on _____ Date _____

Part 2
Which Social Media Platforms are Right for my Business?

*Starting is not
most people's problem,
staying, continuing
and finishing is.*

Darren Hardy

Different Platforms, or 'Socials' for You to Use

I n *Welcome to the Social Media Jungle*, we looked at how so many of us in smaller businesses struggle with effectively using social media as a marketing tool and how so many of us feel that we are on the outside looking in when it comes to using social media. Often, this is why we avoid it because we don't *'get it'. Sound familiar?*

What you post daily will vary depending on the type of business you operate and the social media platform you use. *Oh heck, is 'platform' a new word to you? No problem, that's why you bought this book!* A platform is simply the operating system on which social media is run. In other words, the different social media you have chosen to use for your business. Here we look at which one you might want to focus on for your precious 10 minutes a day. Platforms are also known as *'socials'* – these are one and the same thing.

What platform should you use?

Remember, a platform is the type of social media you want to use to promote your business. There are so many out there and it depends on your personal preferences and who is your *'target market'.*

What do I mean by the target market?

Well, it's about who you want to sell to, your *ideal customer*. People who want to buy and use your product or service.

The platform you choose is REALLY important; say you want to target young, new mums to invest in your 'Getting baby to sleep through the night' course - *that WOULD be a bestseller!* You decide to spend your time posting on LinkedIn or TikTok. However, this wouldn't be the first place young, new mums would look (they are more likely to be using Facebook or Instagram), so your postings have been a huge waste of your time and effort.

Probably, you have got a presence on one or more social media platforms already, which is great and I would encourage you to spend a little time capturing the following information and then just checking where you want to focus your energy. Remember we want to smash this in 10 minutes a day, so make it count.

Your Notes

Where am I spending my social media marketing time at the moment?

_____

How to find my ideal customer to connect with and to promote my business offer?

_____

_____

My ideal customer's gender is: _____

My ideal customer's age is: _____

My ideal customer's location is: _____

_____

Your Notes

Okay let's dig a bit deeper...

Are they employed, self-employed, on leave, looking for work etc?

_____

Describe their family: number of children, close family members etc:

_____

What's their home like? Do they own it, or rent it? Do they live in a rural area, in a city?

_____

What's their income? _____

What are their hobbies?_____

What social media are they on? _____

What time of day are they on it?_____

What do they want and need from you?_____

_____

_____

Any other notes on my ideal customer and who I'd really like to attract to my business:

_____

_____

_____

_____

This short exercise will really help you to focus your time on the right area for your business. Remember this, it's about connecting with *'ideal customers'*, like the one you have outlined above and being online and visible where they are, so you can build a relationship and perhaps help them to buy from you at a later date.

Coach Cath's Top Tip:
Less is More
Do fewer platforms really well
rather than a lot of platforms badly.

It might be that you have a personal, favourite platform that you feel really comfortable with but your target market is elsewhere. So, you can start slow and just pop a small amount of content on their platform and build up your confidence over time. To be honest, most platforms work in a similar way (after all, Facebook own Instagram, Instant Messenger and WhatsApp!), there is a lot of free online training for you on their platforms for you to take advantage of, if you just look for it.

Strength shows not only in the ability to persist, but in the ability to start over.

F. Scott Fitzgerald

My advice at this time would be to choose a maximum of two platforms and allocate 10 minutes a day to each rather than try and do all of them.

Marketing is a subject I won't blow your mind with right now but in *Part 6: Sell Without Selling* I'll give you more tips. For now, let's make sure your precious time is spent where you have the best chance of getting a result.

Here are some very general ideas for you. There is always a wealth of in-depth advice found with a simple Google search, but this is the quick and easy guide, so here are my thoughts!

Remember, no matter WHICH platform you chose; you have to show up consistently.

Your Notes

Which social media platform will I focus on for my marketing activity?

_____

_____

Why is this platform the best for me?

_____

_____

_____

Facebook (FB)

I love Facebook and use it a LOT as a key driver for my coaching business as its demographics match my target audience. Perhaps use this platform if you want to attract a more mature customer as research shows they are still using FB as their main social media platform. Lots of options with profiles, groups, pages, lives, videos, paid adverts etc. Easy to use with its own scheduling tools which can be really helpful.

Facebook Statistics

👍 According to their website at the time of writing 1.66 BILLION people use Facebook worldwide every day and 2.6 BILLION people use it on a monthly basis.

👍 Facebook users spend 38 minutes per day using the platform.

👍 Facebook accounts for over 45 percent of monthly social media visits.

👍 62% of online Seniors aged 65+ are on Facebook and 72% are between age 50-64.

👍 88% of online users aged 18-29 are on Facebook, 84% of those 30-49.

👍 96% of Facebook users accessed via mobile devices.

The art of selling on social media is about connecting with the right people, adding value to their day, and showing off your credibility.

Cath Babbington

The key thing with Facebook is to be focused on where you can get your content in front of your target market. It might be that you have a personal page, a business page and one or more groups on Facebook – each needs its own content and regular information. The more groups or pages you have, the more content you have to put out there, and it has to be different for each group on each day, so again choose wisely.

You have to have a personal account to access FB, they are quite strict on finding out people who are using a personal page as a business page, so be careful of that as FB will close your account down and you could lose everything if you don't *'play by their rules'*. I use mine a lot to share personal stuff but I'm also very aware that I'm out there in front of customers, so nothing inappropriate or negative ever goes on my newsfeed. EVER. *I post daily and try to always show myself as a fun, friendly person you'd like to meet.*

I have a page which I update every other day and treat it like I would a website page. It's where I promote things, tell people about what I'm up to and share content using the planner in this book. You can connect with me at https://www.facebook.com/coachcathuk.

Facebook Groups

A Facebook group is often seen as the ultimate aim as you can then add general connections who match your ideal customer into a group just for you to talk business in. Think about the groups you might be in, some of them have zero content for weeks and others are lively and full of fun – you need to make your group feel like the latter. So again, only do it if you have the time and focus to make it work.

Our greatest weakness lies in giving up.
The most certain way to succeed
is always to try just one more time.

Thomas Edison

If you've been on FB for a while and have got lots of confidence, then go for it, if not maybe use your profile page as a place to get started.

Instagram

Instagram or 'Insta' is another hugely popular social media platform and is owned by Facebook so it's really quite easy to link the two together and save yourself time. Again, it's about doing one thing really well rather than two things half-heartedly so look at these statistics and see where you think your ideal customer will be hanging out and looking for help or to buy.

Insta is a newer social media platform, FB has been around since 2004; Insta is a baby compared to this when it started in 2010.

Instagram Statistics

👍 Total Number of daily active Instagram users across the globe is 500 million + and the number of businesses on Instagram is over 25 million.

👍 56.3% of Instagram users are female and 43.7% are male.

👍 30% of global Instagram audiences were aged between 18 and 24 years and 35 % aged between 25 and 34 years.

👍 72% of teens use Instagram.

👍 70% of shopping enthusiasts turn to Instagram for product discovery.

👍 Photos with Faces Get 38% More Likes.

👍 Posts with at least one hashtag average 12.6% more engagement.

As you can see from the data above, Insta tends to be a younger target market and a more visual platform. Great if you are selling products or services which offer interesting images/videos/lives. Insta is a place for influencers and stories; follow those key people you want to be connected with and engage here. I don't use it that much as it's not my demographic, but I do try to have a presence on Insta to keep my stories and 'grid' reflective of a positive lifestyle. Remember, it's about connecting with your ideal customers, so think about if this is where yours hang out.

Fall seven times, stand up eight.

Japanese Proverb

Instagram TV (IGTV)

This is another way of connecting with people, outside of YouTube with the *'influencers'* and brands using it to help promote their content and build relationships, as it is:

- ✦ Targeted to mobile viewers.

- ✦ Video displays vertically.

- ✦ Starts playing automatically when the Instagram app is in use.

- ✦ Option to comment and share with friends.

- ✦ Features content from people the user already follows.

- ✦ Videos appear in the user's newsfeed.

- ✦ Anyone can create content for IGTV.

LinkedIn (LI)

Seen as the *'professional network'* some people say you can sell anything on this platform but for me this is a more business to business (B2B) option and so it's useful if your ideal customer is employed for themselves or in an organisation. That's not to say if you're selling a product and not a service it won't get seen there, most people on LI are *'lurkers'*. Being a *'lurker'* means they see you on there but don't comment or engage with you until they want something from you. There's a HUGE reach of people on LI, just have a look at the statistics below.

Basic LinkedIn is free to use and adequate for most usage. I think if you're looking at business to business marketing to a professional customer base, this is where you could spend your time most effectively.

LinkedIn Statistics

  ♣ Total Number of LinkedIn users is 675 million, with a total number monthly active users 310 million.

  ♣ There are 57% of male users and 43% female users on LinkedIn.

  ♣ 24% of Millennials (23-38 years old) use LinkedIn.

  ♣ LinkedIn is the #1 channel B2B marketers use to distribute content at 94%.

  ♣ An average user spends 17 minutes monthly on LinkedIn.

  ♣ LinkedIn profiles with professional headshots get 14 times more profile views.

It would perhaps be fair to say on this platform it's less of the funny selfies of your dog and more of the expert posts and solving problems content. LinkedIn is unusual in that you can *'cluster post'* i.e. put multiple different posts on at the same time, as it is so massive they never follow in a thread type pattern and been seen in sequence; this is a win if you're very busy and want to get it all done in one go. Live streaming and video work well too although if you can use captions on video feeds, more people are likely to watch them. You may need to make a LinkedIn application in order to use the Live option!

Showing off industry expertise and knowledge really builds your credibility on LinkedIn, so always make sure you share this whenever possible.

LinkedIn is seen as the Business to Business platform however, with the right content you can sell anything on LinkedIn!

Cath Babbington

Just like other social media platforms you can have a personal profile and a business/company page, and these are free too. A lot of people have both and use the Business Page as a type of website to signpost people to your business and perhaps having a clearer sales message on there. Again, this does mean that you have two areas to update. I'd suggest the personal profile has to be updated daily, perhaps more so and the business page could be three times a week. However, if you want to do it in 10 minutes a day, focus on your personal profile only.

I find that the harder I work, the more luck I seem to have.

Thomas Jefferson, Founding Father and President of the United States

---

Pinterest

This is another visual platform, so big on the images, photos, displays, staging and flatlays, (which are styled photo's that display your product in an attractive setting)Pinterest experts use a range of effects to really show off their products to their best. It's often seen as the platform you go to first if you want to buy something a little more interesting or unique, so if this is your market you need to be here.

Pinterest Statistics

👍 The total Number of monthly active Pinterest users is 335 million+ with a total number of Pinterest Pins at 200 billion and the current number of Pinterest Boards at a huge 4 billion.

👍 71% of Pinterest users are actually female.

👍 The median age of a Pinterest user is 40, however, the majority of active pinners are below the age of 40.

👍 28% of marketers are already using Pinterest. 83% of weekly pinners have made a purchase based on content they saw from brands on Pinterest.

👍 47% Social media users saw Pinterest as the platform for discovering and shopping for products.

👍 72% of Pinners use Pinterest to decide what to buy offline.

If you can't fly then run.
If you can't run, then walk.
And, if you can't walk, then crawl,
but whatever you do, you have to
keep moving forward.

Martin Luther King Jnr

People who use this platform are called pinners and they create an online *'photo album'* or pinboard of their products by *'pinning'* them on there. *So it's called pinning, not posting, get it?* Pinners use these pin boards to show off their products and create a gallery of images for people to look through in their newsfeed. This is a little different to other platforms but is easy to use once you get the hang of it.

Don't be a pushy salesperson on whatever
platform you are on, offer good and
varied content, help out others,
be kind and show off your stuff.

Cath Babbington

You can have a business or personal account, and you get statistics with the business account, which is always useful. It's really important that you have a great profile that shows off your best *'pins'* so that people want to look at your content and follow you.

Remember to be transparent with your pricing too. (If people are unsure, they will click elsewhere rather than buy from you.)

You can use links to drive people to your website or online shop for direct selling.

Snapchat

Is Snapchat a social media platform you can market from or is it a messaging site? Maybe these statistics will help you understand if this could be an area you can connect with your ideal customer?

A *'snap'* is a picture or video (max 10 seconds) you send through to your friends and once viewed it is automatically deleted unless the receiver adds it to their story so it can be shared with all your friends. Snapchat is effectively split into two areas. The first is your friends (on the left of your screen), and these are the people that you message and connect with every day. The right-hand side of the screen is called *'discover'* and this is where users connect with brands, influencers and is an area you can potentially market from.

Snapchat Statistics

Total Number of monthly active users is 360 million and the total Number of daily active Snapchat users is a whopping 218 million.

   ☛ 78% of internet users aged 18-24 use Snapchat.

   ☛ 90% of Snapchat users are 13-24 years old.

   ☛ Roughly 61% of Snapchat users are female and 38% are male.

   ☛ Time spent among Snapchat's adult users per day is 28 minutes.

Like so many other platforms it offers a business account which may help you market your products and services. It can be especially useful if you are targeting a younger demographic who often *'impulse'* buy. This platform is very different from others and you might decide to use your '*regular*' platform to share the fact you're on Snapchat to start to get followers. You can also create a '*SnapCode*' which is similar to a QR code and helps people follow you easily.

Perhaps not for people new to social media marketing at first, but definitely worth a try and if your target customer is in the younger age group, then it's really worth adding it to your social media mix, perhaps once you have your more familiar platform up and running smoothly.

> *Don't count the days,*
> *make the days count.*
>
> Muhammad Ali

TikTok

This platform is still emerging and is very much seen as a young person's platform for taking and viewing videos. Just LOOK at the numbers it has though...

TikTok Statistics

👍 Total Number of monthly active users are an amazing 800 million with a total number of TikTok downloads at an astonishing 1,65 million and the number of video views per day come in at 1 billion.

👍 If your market is China or India, then TikTok is the place to be!

👍 41 percent of TikTok users are aged 16-24.

👍 56% of TikTok users are male, 44% are female.

👍 TikTok's average engagement rate is 29%.

👍 4% of social media marketers use the platform.

TikTok is seen as the fun social media, it's rare to see a massive amount of business content on there. I suspect this will change and future versions of this book will have more ideas on how to use TikTok for pure business marketing BUT if you sell teen products, have a dance school or like to show yourself to a new market, then give it a try. *Be aware your kids may hate you for it!*

As you develop your video feed, you'll find the platform picks up on the ones you like the most, so you can get more of what you want very quickly. There is an emerging amount of content on videos which target *'quick tips'* or ideas that could easily support a business focus.

If you really look closely, most overnight successes took a long time.

Steve Jobs

Just like any video platform, it does take a bit of time to create, edit and perfect the TikTok videos, even if they're only 14 or 60 seconds long, so perhaps consider whether this is the first platform you could use or if your 10 minutes a day might be better off spent elsewhere – for now. I love looking though it and it makes me laugh, so if nothing else waste a few minutes every week keeping in touch with this vibrant and fast-growing platform.

Coach Cath's Top Tip:
Remember you are online
to create content not to
be hooked into others' content!

Twitter

Twitter was created as a social media platform back in 2006 and is now seen as a way to instantly communicate with a network across the world. A tweet is the content you post and it's limited to 140 words. It is a very busy platform and the life-span of a tweet is in seconds, not in minutes so visibility is a real challenge. If you already tweet and have a good base, the more the merrier is something that you can really benefit from.

Twitter Statistics

👍 Total number of monthly active Twitter users is 330 million with a massive Tweets sent per day of over 500 million!

👍 Twitter users are 34% female and 66% male.

👍 Roughly 42% of Twitter users are on daily.

👍 80% of Twitter users are affluent millennials.

👍 85% of small and medium business users use Twitter to provide customer service.

👍 Tweets with GIFs get 55% more engagement than those without. However, only 2% of Tweets contain GIFs.

A year from now you may
wish you had started today.

Karen Lamb

Most tweets tend to be newsworthy and contain information. What some people consider news, others may not, and you do need to be very responsive on this network to get noticed. If you have a professional B2B or

B2C business, perhaps a lawyer or financial advisor for example, this could be a great way of sharing lots of business news and getting your credibility sky high by networking with others also in the field. Like all social media, people will watch you, make a connection and then get in touch when they need you.

Be aware that people often *'vent'* on Twitter in a way that is sometimes faster moving than on other platforms. Posts, comments and negative news can *'go viral'* before there is time to react to it, something to consider if you are looking at just 10 minutes activity once a day.

YouTube

This platform is owned by Google and many *'people in the know'* suggest that it could be their next big business growth area. It's now the second *'search engine'* next to Google, used by typing in a general subject and receiving lots of suggestions. *They certainly have this part of the internet nailed!*

YouTube Statistics

Total number of monthly active YouTube users ramp up to a massive 2 billion with the total Number of daily active YouTube users coming in at 30 million.

- 👍 62% of YouTube users are male.

- 👍 62% of businesses use YouTube.

- 👍 9% of small businesses are on YouTube.

- 👍 YouTube is the 2nd most visited site in the world.

- 👍 YouTube attracts about 44% of all internet users.

To be frank with you, I'm unsure if it's a *'quick win'* that you can do in just 10 minutes a day, for me this is a space where a simple *'home made'* video which you use your phone for and pop on without editing just isn't going to make you stand out for the right reasons. In 10 minutes, a day it's not possible BUT if it's the platform you need then the daily planners will still work – it'll just take you a little longer to produce great content.

Coach Cath's Top Tip:
Less is More
Post consistently on the same platform people will create their own habit and look out for YOUR new content.

Actions to take

  ☙ Make sure you're spending your time on the right platform for your business. You need to be where your ideal customers are.

  ☙ Make sure any pages, groups, or profiles you have are all up to date.

  ☙ Go through them and make sure they represent your business.

  ☙ Consider using the same profile picture across all platforms, if you decide to use more than one, as it helps with the *'brand image'*. I personally like to see the person, not the logo on social media. I feel that *'people buy from people'*, not logo's, BUT if you're really shy, then that's okay.

  ☙ Delete any unprofessional, very personal, or potentially inappropriate posts from your history; its time to start afresh.

👍 Think about archiving any platforms you are not going to focus on right now. If you make them inactive, that is so much better than leaving it out there looking sad and unused. You can always go back to it at a later date once you have sorted out one platform at a time?

👍 If your spelling is poor, consider typing up your content on word then you can check it before you pop it on your profile. Most people expect the odd typo, but your 'about me' information must be flawless.

👍 Researching people who are *'influencers'* or well known in your areas is always a good idea, if you get ideas on how they work, just by following them, that's great.

👍 If you're unsure what engaging content should look like, search through 'the competition' and see what they're doing. *Don't copy it, that's not on at all*, but note it gives you an idea on how you could present your page, group, stories, or profiles.

👍 Try to connect with and follow industry experts from your field of work, so that you can keep up to date with what the latest news, trends and favourites are and reflect them on your own profiles. Commenting regularly on their posts can add to your credibility too.

The customers WILL come when you're consistently connecting with them!

Please note all statistics in this chapter are sourced from www.omnicoreagency.com.

Part 3
Different Types of
Social Media Posts

*The value of an idea
lies in the using of it.*

Thomas Edison

What the heck do I do every day?

For so many people, the consistency of posting daily on their social media is where it's easy to come unstuck. Finding new content for some people is easy, you see them pop up all the time and think, wow, that's great. Try not to compare yourself to others, if they are a *'big fish'* it's highly likely most of it will be from a professional copywriter or some of their team who's got a degree in marketing and paid to do their online stuff.

You're not like that, you have 10 minutes a day to be visible and credible to your chosen market, so it's about maintaining the *flywheel effect* and getting traction by just getting on with it without overthinking!

Applied knowledge is power and power is confidence! But first let's look at the words used on various platforms and to remind you what they mean:

Followers - these are people who you have connected with and follow your social media posts. You'll probably see the same people crop up time after time. The idea is to get as many people *'following you'* who match your ideal customer profile. Don't just add loads of people endlessly, be more focused and add people to your network who are likely to want to hear from you and respond to you.

Views - this is how many people, either from your network or outside of it, who see your post.

The more views you have the better, as it gets your content out there. Most social platforms like to see lots of views, so mixing up your content, keeping it fresh and different daily is key to increasing the number of views.

Engagement - this is when people like, love, or better still, comment and react to your post. Getting high engagement is as important as views as it shows that you're connecting with your target customer and encouraging them to respond. Some people are controversial on purpose to get engagement, it's a too high-risk strategy for me, but going back to posts and commenting on others' reaction is important – no one likes to be ignored!

Hashtag - the hashtag is this sign # and it's used on all sorts of different platforms. Hashtags were first introduced by Twitter where you will see them a lot and also on LinkedIn and on Instagram.

Whenever you add a # to your content, it then becomes searchable by others, which is important as it helps your content get seen. Indeed on some platforms, such as Instagram. If you don't # then you are going to struggle to get your message out there.

There is some skill to using the correct # so here are some tips for you:

✑ Do not use any punctuation. Note: it's #businesscoaching, not #business.coaching so make sure the formatting is correct or it could mean something different and not as intended.

✍ Try to be specific with your #Hashtag, it's a very busy world out there. For example, if you post #business then it's probable your post will be lost in the masses. If you can be more specific and post #smallbusinessstartups you're more likely to get more views, therefore more traction. There are loads of search engines out there that can help with this, maybe start small and simple and as you gain confidence, do more ambitious hashtags.

✍ If you create your own business hashtag, do make sure it's not already in use by someone else or all of your hard work is helping them not you and you might upset a fellow social media connection, which you do not want. If you do go for it, make it easy to spell.

✍ Use the hashtags in your actual content rather than just sticking them in at the end. Like this:

> Today's great session of #smallbusinesscoaching with my latest customer #coffeehousecares was a huge success. I love spending time with #favcustomers.

Rather than:

> Today's great session of coaching with my latest customer at our local coffee house was a huge success. I love spending time with favourite customers. #smallbusinesscoaching #coffeehousecares #favcustomers.

Do as others do is a great idea to build up your experience. Look at businesses similar to yours and see what hashtags they're using, then try out the same ones. Please don't copy like for like, but if there are some great ideas for hashtags that you might benefit from them, it's a good way to build confidence in the early days.

Number of hashtags used on social media platforms

Facebook ## - use 2 hashtags per post.

There is a lot of conflicting commentary on whether or not to use hashtags on Facebook and I think it is only useful if you have content elsewhere what uses a regular hashtag and then it creates a brand for you across all social media platforms. I'd also suggest if you have a certain geography or linking to a specific social trend such as #pride or #blacklivesmatter then that can be powerful too, but on the whole, don't go shoving in lots of hashtags, it just isn't really done on FB and clutters up your content and maybe does more harm than good.

Twitter # or #.

Use 1-2 hashtags per post maximum. If you are a local business, try to use location-specific hashtags to increase your reach and engagement.

Twitter is the site that introduced the hashtag feature so it's pretty key to being seen on this platform. Using trends and themes with the hashtag is also key as Twitter is seen as the key place to get up to date news, so using a relevant hashtag shows your credibility.

Instagram ######### - use 9+ hashtags per post.
Insta (alongide Twitter) is where the use of hashtags is key to visibility Insta is THE place to go crazy, however, some research I've read suggests 9 # is the best option for maximum engagement. However, even adding just one alone can up your content by around 10%, so again you can start small and build up. Other research says go to the max with 30, so do what works for you but do include at least one hashtag with every post, either in the comments or in the photo or video caption.

Hashtags can sometimes be banned, which means if you're using one that is, your content is going nowhere. As always being more specific with your hashtagging will help you avoid this, as will following others and see what hashtags they are using.

Instagram stores can also have hashtags, up to ten. Remember to start small and try to be specific with the ones you choose.

Pinterest ### - use 3 hashtags per post.
This platform isn't massively about the hashtag, so you don't have to go too mad. Use of them tends to be limited to the actual Pin description so that's always a great place to pop in the odd hashtag, especially if you have a specific product campaign, such as Christmas gifts or new lines to highlight.

LinkedIn #### - use 3-4 hashtags.
Whilst LinkedIn isn't known for its prolific use of the hashtag, they can help you reach a specific audience, especially if you're publishing an article or joining a specific debate. As with Twitter and Facebook, location - specific hashtags work well.

LinkedIn offers users the option to follow certain hashtags so can be useful in keeping you in touch with the latest news and trends in your field and so enhances your knowledge and credibility.

TikTok #########- use 9 per video.

TikTok loves a hashtag! It's wise to get this right to ensure your video content is seen. As before you can just type in the #symbol and enter a phrase with no spaces. If you want to explore the latest hashtags, go into the discover option on your screen and just scroll through and use whichever one meets your needs. Trends change daily on TikTok so it's wise to be up to date if you can but there don't seem to be too many hard and fast rules in this relatively new platform, so feel free to go with it.

Your Notes

What relevant business hashtags could I use to maximise views on social media?

_____

_____

_____

_____

_____

_____

_____

_____

_____

YouTube ##### - use 5 to 9 hashtags maximum.
With so many people using YouTube every day it's another platform where the careful use of hashtags can help your content gain visibility. Try to use hashtags in the titles and descriptions of your videos to get the maximum visibility, always be specific and don't go crazy.

If using a # looks as if they could be really important for you, try a special site for more information on which # will match your specific business needs. I use https://hashtagify.me but there are loads out there with a simple Google search.

The fastest way to change yourself
is to hang out with people who are
already the way you want to be.

Reid Hoffman

TOP TIPS

Using emojis - these are often useful to break up paragraphs into chunks and perhaps add themes to your post. These vary per post and platform, but I like them a lot as they are eye-catching whereas only using text isn't!

Frequency of posting - as already mentioned, showing up everywhere every day is key to your success, but reuse, repurpose and mix up your content over different platforms on different days if you can as it saves time and effort. Don't however, just post identical content at the same time everywhere unless it's on someone ELSE's page (networking groups for example).

Groups, pages, and other stuff - each platform has its different ways of working, for example, on Facebook you can have a profile, a page, and a group and multiples of these.

So, maximise your coverage BUT you must then do more content and more posting so think hard before you try and do too much quantity. Remember consistency is key and 10 minutes a day is the target.

Adding/inviting/tagging people - social media is a busy world so there is a lot of competition for attention, especially if your business operates in a crowded market. Add/invite/tag the right people to ensure you reach your ideal customer. Friends and family add numbers and often support you in the beginning, however adding and tagging people you want to respond is a better medium-term plan. In the longer term, they will request to be added and tag you!

Algorithms - you'll no doubt have heard this word and maybe don't understand what it means to your social media content. An algorithm is a sort of inbuilt code that tracks user content on each different social media platform. Each platform has its own algorithm and they are constantly changing. If you are a tech genius this would be something to dig deeper into, but we want results in 10 minutes a day, so the strategy this book teaches is visibility, consistency, and variety of content that gets you out there and drives reach & engagement. *Stick with the plan and don't worry about the technical stuff!*

Timing of Posts - in general, just posting every day is the target, no matter what the time is but it can be quite useful to make a mental note of what posts get a reaction and to see if there is a particular time of the day or in the evening where you get a lot more engagement than others. For example, I find my target audience tend to be online later in the evening, so posts that I put on later get a better response.

Your Notes

What's specific to my social media?

_____

_____

_____

_____

Types of Posts and Terms Used

It would be helpful for you to understand the terms we are using and how each sort of different post works before we get into the monthly planner.

Depending on your chosen platform and the type of business you have will define what makes the magic work for you. Don't feel overwhelmed as you continue to go through this chapter.

This is a guide to the typical posts that you see all over any platform and these are all included in the planners across each month so don't feel obliged to memorise all of this information, but some understanding will help build your knowledge.

Start off sticking to the planners and then feel free to do something different, which meets the needs of your ideal customer and business.

Once you have decided what platform you are using, you can mix and match to your heart's desire, there is often overlap so do what's right for you and mix it up to keep it interesting, and fresh.

Social media needs to reflect you and your business, if you are in a visual market, then the posts that reflect this on Insta and Pinterest will be more successful for you. If you are a Business to Business (B2B) service, then it's likely that credibility posts and sharing industry news on LinkedIn are a better option.

If you're unsure, go back to *Part 2 - How to find my Ideal Customer* and check out who your ideal customer is and where they are spending most of their time.

Affinity Post - this type of post can be long or short, but it's about showing that you understand your followers' pain and empathise with it (and how you can solve it too maybe?) These posts share some personal stuff about the challenges you have in a situation and are there to create a personal bond with your followers.

Ask a Question - similar to the CTA below, but often on the back of a current topic, so things like, is it snowing where you are or what is the one thing that annoys you the most, etc. These are easy to do BUT try to tag followers in them so you get a response, otherwise it looks like no one is interested if you get no comments.

Blogs *(if you write one, share it everywhere)* - not everyone blogs or writes articles but if you do then it makes sense to share the content of the links to everyone on every platform. These often work well on a Friday as many people are often quieter towards the weekend, and if it's interesting, they will look over the weekend. This can also drive traffic to your website.

Call to Action (CTA) - some business owners feel uncomfortable about this, but it plays a strong part in any social media communication. It's around putting something in front of your followers and asking them to take action. This is often for a promotion on a product or service, perhaps when there is a deadline. Special offers/sign up here/ complete a poll/tell me what you think... All of these are calls to action that you can scatter in with other posts. *Don't bombard though, use wisely.*

Competitions *(if appropriate, go for it)* - again, this depends on your business and I'm not a great one for offering FREE things, as people can come to expect them, which is not good for sales. However, a monthly prize draw, recognition of regular engagement, or occasional competition is always a winner if it's something your customer and potential customer value.

Expert - an expert post takes a bit longer but is important to do as often as you can. This is where you show off your expertise in your business area. Give meaningful tips or advice, show what you can do to help your customers. Show off your in-depth knowledge so people see you as the number one expert in your chosen field.

Lives - a *'live'* is when you are using a video stream in a live situation straight on your social media platform and direct to your followers. It's not available on every platform but is one of my favourites as they can be done anytime, anyplace, and anywhere.

They do make people nervous at the start, but you can have a practice and just use the delete option if you don't want to publish it. If you tell people you're new to live streaming, they will often engage more and tell you they loved it, so that's a real boost.

Coach Cath's Top Tip:

Lives and videos can be nerve-wracking when you first start them, but are a sure-fire way of reaching and connecting with your audience; don't be shy, go for it. Practice makes perfect.
– Just show up and do it!

Always title them and try not to waffle on, maybe have a little note with key messages and I like to keep them short and sweet to start with.

Once you feel more comfortable, you can do a longer *'live'* for a targeted audience. Many social media influencers do this and have a regular weekly time slot where they connect with their followers and offer great content, ideas, and offers direct to them. *It's a real winner and, I suspect, will become even more in the next year, so give it a go!*

Long Post - these seem to be different on different platforms and take some more thinking. They are longer than a usual post and tell a business or personal 'story' again to either build empathy or explain how you can help others. These need more thought to make sure they are interesting enough to keep your followers' attention.

Meme/Quotes - these are great, loads are available but don't rely solely on them. They need some content to explain what the message means – did it make you think/laugh/cry/reflect etc. You'll often see people on social media use a meme every day with zero thought and then they wonder why their marketing isn't working. A meme with relevance is great, an inspirational quote is, well, inspirational but do use the planner and use sparingly.

Coach Cath's Top Tip:
Always remember people buy from people not stock images and memes!

News/What's Trending - these sorts of posts are around the latest updates concerning your product or service. Similar to an expert post but shows that your knowledge is current, and you are on top of anything your followers might need to or want to know about. Comment and share any articles, expert posts, or things that show your audience you are up to date and on-trend.

Try to avoid too much commentary on areas that could be considered controversial, such as politics, unless this is your area of expertise, as this is a sure-fire way of losing some followers, or annoying others!

Product Visuals - if you are selling a product you need to use visuals of them frequently, again don't just stick a stock photo and expect people to buy, if you can use a real photo of you or others with your product too, present it well and explain why they need to have it. Try to be upfront and transparent with pricing. You don't go shopping at the supermarket without a quick price check – it's the same on social media – make it easy for them to buy from you.

Selfies - selfies are awesome as they let people see who you are and what you look like – we are all nosey! Selfies can be at work, with others, social posts, or just funny things you've seen that day – these are very quick and easy. Get the camera angle up high, use a filter if you want, and try to make it about a topic, not just a photo stuck on your feed. Let people into your business life and do your selfie in a work-based context.

Service Visuals - similar to above, post your service frequently and use images of what you do, preferably with you in them. Explain your service in simple terms and again be as transparent as possible with your pricing without losing your competitive edge.

Share Yourself *(share something personal)* - this is a personal choice, some people love posting about their family, friends' dogs, etc, and others less so. Do what's right for you but try not to use your kids or friends as a constant marketing tool unless this is your market and you're 100% happy to do so. Your choice here.

Please note – PETS – some people love them, some people hate them - but a cute puppy, kitten or exotic animal is often a marketing opportunity from heaven!

Coach Cath's Top Tip:
Over time you will find out which types of
posts are your favourite and get the most
engagement from your followers,
so max up on these if you can –
if something's working, do more of it!

Surveys and Polls - most platforms allow you to do
polls and it's a sure-fire way of getting engagement
on a post if your poll catches the imagination.
Asking people what they need, want, or like about
a product, service or situation is also very useful
marketing research.

Testimonials - a massive win on all platforms.
Ask every customer to give you a testimonial and
then share it. *Terry Pratchett once said "too much
punctuation is the sign of an unbalanced mind (!!!)"*
Screengrab a comment, copy an email, re-post
positive posts to your followers and generally show
everyone what your existing customers like and
how you have benefitted them. Remember, if you're
showing any personal information, make sure
everyone is happy for you to do so.

Videos - a video post is simply a video you have
made, usually quite short, that you can put on most
social media platforms. You can do a video on your
business, your offer, or your products. Lots of people
use them as a demonstration for a product as it's
often better to show people what something does
rather than tell them. A simple video uploaded from
your phone is good enough for most platforms.

If you're nervous on camera, this is a safer way to start, and with mobile phones, tablets, and laptops all having built-in cameras and microphones, it's an easy way to get your message out there. Videos are said to have up to 50% more engagement than other posts, so well worth the effort. Also, one video can be posted on multiple platforms and so you get great coverage for just one little video. If you are techy, adding sub-titles is even better to increase more views and helps those with hearing issues connect with you too.

Just like doing a live, have a structure, what you are going to tell your connections and what's in it for them to listen to you?

Coach Cath's Top Tip:
Do what works for you. Remember it's all about visibility AND consistency, then content.

If you're new to this, just use the planner for each month to guide you, OR choose four different types of posts that YOU feel happy with and focus on them. For example, if you hate doing videos or lives, don't go there yet - use a longer post instead.

If you've got a lot of great images of a specific offer or activity, then go mad on that for a week.

Your Notes

What posts do I feel comfortable with?

_____

_____

_____

What type of content might I struggle with?

_____

_____

_____

What can I learn from this chapter?

_____

_____

_____

_____

_____

_____

_____

_____

_____

_____

Social media is here.
It's not going away; not a passing fad.
Be where your customers are:
in social media.

Lori Ruff, Speaker and Author

Part 4
Quick Success
Monthly Planner

*Social media is the ultimate equalizer.
It gives a voice and a platform to
anyone willing to engage.*

Amy Jo Martin

January

There is a lot going on in January, so, the biggest opportunities are out there for you. Think of the traditional *'January Sale'* of products or services, it's time to 'go to town' and post daily or a few times a day, especially in the first two weeks.

Another strong theme for January is: New Year's Resolutions and making changes in your life. Most small businesses can capitalise on this marketing opportunity; this is your time to build relationships and show people what you can do to help them. Everything from mental health, diet and fitness, new hobbies, different ways of doing things, CHANGE, and how you can support and facilitate that change is a biggy.

Chinese New Year (sometimes in February) can be another opportunity for you, again you can link your services and products to this with some thought (even if there isn't something immediately obvious). Showing an awareness of global celebrations, issues and cultures can be a great chance to connect with people on a deeper level, so pencil in the actual date and go for it.

Other marketing opportunities which have the same date every year are in the planner itself.

January

1	**New Year's Day** Share with your customers your New Year Resolutions.	**2**	January sale of service or products! (include CTA).
5	Selfie of you at work with or using products.	**6**	Share a statistic relating to your business.
9	Ask an engagement question, use a poll or meme to help you.	**10**	Use a quote related to your business.
13	Showcase how your services or products help people.	**14**	Share Knowledge. Post a link of your favourite article.
17	Use a funny or thought-provoking quote related to your business.	**18**	Showcase your latest offer. (include CTA).
21	Out and about, share what you are up to with a selfie.	**22**	Introduce Valentine's Day offers! (advance notice
25	**Burns Night** Give a suggestion in 'Rabbie Burns' Style!	**26**	**Australia Day** Share a business story themed to this da
29	Share favourite resources you use in your business.	**30**	Ask an engagement question.

Blue Monday - a day of gloom falls in January - Post something fun to cheer people up.

January

3 Share a testimonial from a customer.	**4** VIDEO – show customers what your business can offer them (include CTA).
7 Long post – all about how you love your business.	**8** Expert post show off your knowledge and build credibility.
11 GO LIVE – talk about your business (include CTA).	**12** Share a 'fill in the gap' post!
15 VIDEO – show customers how you add value.	**16** Share a selfie relating to your business.
19 Long story post about how January has been for your business so far.	**20** Share a memorable experience.
23 GO LIVE – talk about what blows your mind about your business.	**24** Thank a customer, friend, or contact – tag them and big them up.
27 **Holocaust Day of Commemoration** Post something related.	**28** More on Valentine's Day offers if you're buying or selling (include CTA).
31 Share how you have kept your New Year Resolutions!	

Down Syndrome Awareness Month, National Book Month, Pizza Week (2nd Week), Peculiar People Day (10th).

Your Notes

Specific content ideas for January:

_____

_____

_____

_____

_____

_____

_____

_____

_____

_____

_____

_____

_____

_____

_____

_____

_____

_____

_____

_____

_____

February

This month is another golden opportunity for many businesses to link to the theme of LOVE, relationships, friendship, and Valentine's Day. Even if you don't have a direct link, such as beauty products or flowers to sell, there are a host of opportunities to market around self-care, loving children, and reaching out to extended families or friends you haven't seen for a while.

Pancake Day changes every year, so get the date in the calendar and have some fun with it – a video of you making and trying to toss a pancake is sure to be a winner, or maybe doing a pancake race in the garden, your connections will love something to giggle at in the middle of winter, *trust me!*

February is the shortest month of the year but in the UK and Northern hemisphere is often the gloomiest one, so people are indoors, feeling glum and looking at bad weather every day. Continue with the positive and consistent themes, don't allow your content to become dreary or negative.

February

1	Valentine's Day reminder – share your offers (more if you're selling).	**2**	**Groundhog Day (USA)** Post a repeat!
5	VIDEO – show customers how you add value (include CTA).	**6**	Use a meme - link to your business and to the 'LOVE' theme
9	Flashback - Share previous Valentine Day experiences.	**10**	Long story post why you 'LOVE' your business.
13	GO LIVE – talk about why you 'LOVE' your customers.	**14**	**Valentine's Day** Show some engaging visuals!
17	Post a thought-provoking quote related to your business.	**18**	Out and about, share a usual day with a work-based selfie
21	Build credibility, give a top tip from your business or sector.	**22**	GO LIVE – talk about the weather, economy, or other new
25	Have a flashback day, what were you doing this time last year?	**26**	Put links out to articles you have written or like.
29	Long post on what's new in your business next month.		

Valentine's Day is celebration of love and friendship and was originally a Spring Festival.

February

Share your most romantic moment (affinity post).	**4** **World Cancer Day (Global)** Post something related.
GO LIVE – talk about your business & any promo (include CTA).	**8** Valentine's Day coming soon. Show people you love them!
Share a funny experience about Valentine's Day.	**12** Give offers for Valentine's Day or share someone else's.
VIDEO – show how you celebrated Valentine's Day.	**16** Share a testimonial from a customer, who loves working with you.
Share a FAQ about your business.	**20** Share a silly and fun video.
Share some news to keep your contacts interested in you.	**24** Showcase your products or services (include a CTA).
Share a memorable experience of being in business.	**28** Give a testimonial for a customer or contact and tag them.

Bird Feeding Month, Safer Internet Day (7th), National Chip Week, Fair Trade fortnight.

Your Notes

Specific content ideas for February:

_____

_____

_____

_____

_____

_____

_____

_____

_____

_____

_____

_____

_____

_____

_____

_____

_____

_____

_____

March

Gosh! So much to go for in March, as usual, the fixed date ideas are built into the planner, so do remember to use these on the specific day and try to make them relevant to you and your business.

In March we have the coming of Spring and frequently Mother's Day (UK) falls in March, and sometimes Easter. All of these are big social media content themes regardless of whether your service or product links into them, but you can usually make a link, be it holidays with the children off school. In the same way as Valentine's Day, follow a theme of love, family, friendship and self-care if you're a parent around Mother's Day – you can get lots of ideas from just this one event alone.

Easter is a Christian festival but often revolves around chocolate and family days rather than the actual story of Easter, so know your market and share what's appropriate.

Weather is ALWAYS a good option if you get stuck, it's a great quick fix for content ideas – driving to a customer in the snow, getting soaked as you post your products off, feeling chilly as you sit at your desk or enjoying a sunny walk and doing a '*live*' outside.

March

1	**St David's Day (Wales)** Post something relevant.	**2**	GO LIVE – talk about your business (include CTA).
5	Thank and big up a customer you've worked with recently.	**6**	Long story post about you at this time of year.
9	GO LIVE – talk about your business and what you've been up to.	**10**	Recommend a product you use and say why you like it!
13	Create a poll about your sector.	**14**	VIDEO – show customers how they can buy from you.
17	**St Patrick's Day** Post something business related.	**18**	Out and about, share what you are up to with a selfie.
21	**First Day of Spring** Share what you are up to with a selfie.	**22**	Mother's Day (UK) Take a Selfie with a Mum you admire.
25	VIDEO – tell customers why Mums are important for the world.	**26**	GO LIVE – talk about your business (include a CTA).
29	Share a statistic relating to your business.	**30**	Show customers how you add value to them.

Mother's Day UK is always held on the 4th Sunday of Lent, whereas USA celebrate the day in May.

March

3 Showcase your services or products and any special offers.	**4** VIDEO – show customers how you understand their needs.
7 Share a 'fill in the gap' post, funny works best.	**8** **International Women's Day** Share a woman's story.
11 Selfie of you with a customer.	**12** Expert post – show off your knowledge and build credibility.
15 Share some gossip about your business to prove you're up-to-date!	**16** Do a long post about how your month is going.
19 Share a memorable experience (affinity with customers).	**20** Share a testimonial from a customer, and express your thanks.
23 Share links of people whose social media posts you enjoy.	**24** Thank a customer, friend, or contact – tag them and big them up.
27 Do a weather post! Any you like!	**28** Have a flashback day – what were you doing a year ago?
31 Have a long post. Highlight your March activities and future plans.	

trition Month. World Book Day, World Maths Day, Smoking Day (check dates yearly). Clocks Go Forward.

Your Notes

Specific content ideas for March:

_____

_____

_____

_____

_____

_____

_____

_____

_____

_____

_____

_____

_____

_____

_____

_____

_____

_____

_____

_____

_____

_____

April

Depending on the specific yearly dates, you can continue or start with the marketing for Easter; do feel confident in selling products and services. Remember, social media marketing is a form of 'Sell without Selling', so use it as part of your content mix rather than everything you put out there.

Ramadan is a religious period for the Muslim community that often falls into this time of year, and is a much bigger timeline, as the Muslim population fast for 40 days and follow practices such as sharing, kind acts, thoughtfulness, and love in a way most people don't realise; show empathy and knowledge of this community and open up new ways to connect with customers.

Build relationships, share with customers how you are the ONE person who understands them, and they can relate to. As you connect more over time, you will create a firmer sales platform. After all, if they don't need your product or service right now, they might do so in the future and you want to be the first port of call for your customers.

April 1st is known as April Fool's Day in 11 countries, just remember that humour can be of individual taste so be careful not to offend anyone with your fool's post.

April

1	**April Fool's Day** Share a funny joke, image or story.	**2**	GO LIVE - talk excitedly about your business.
5	Share your latest offers (include a CTA).	**6**	Share resources you find helpful in your specific field of work.
9	Share your latest offers.	**10**	Expert post to show your knowledge and build credibility.
13	Share a business story or a personal photo.	**14**	Showcase your products or services (include a CTA).
17	Long story post about why you started your business.	**18**	VIDEO - show how you interact and support customers.
21	Expert post-show off your knowledge and build credibility.	**22**	Selfie of you at work.
25	GO LIVE - talk about your business (include a CTA).	**26**	Share a news article relating to your business.
29	Give a statistic relating to your business.	**30**	Share a memorable day from this month.

Easter often falls in April.

April

3 GO LIVE – talk about what's been happening in your business.	**4** Showcase your products or services with images (include CTA).
7 **World Health Day** Post something related to business health.	**8** Discuss a statistic relating to your business.
11 VIDEO – show customers your offers, products or services (include CTA).	**12** Share some tips - how you self-care and look after yourself.
15 Give a testimonial about someone in your network, share the love.	**16** Share a 'fill in the gap' post, the sillier the better!
19 Out and about, share what you are up to with a selfie.	**20** Show customers how your business adds value to their lives?
23 **St Georges Day (England)** Post something related.	**24** Share your best success story from your life/business.
27 Thank a customer – tag them and big them up.	**28** Share your latest offers (include CTA).

National Pet Month.

Your Notes

Specific content ideas for April:

_____

_____

_____

_____

_____

_____

_____

_____

_____

_____

_____

_____

_____

_____

_____

_____

_____

_____

_____

_____

_____

May

May has the theme of holidays for the UK as there are both Bank Holidays and School Holidays this month. The weather should be warming up too, so it's a great theme to use for outdoor fun, activities, and lifestyle content. If you're not in the UK, I suspect a similar theme will work just as well and give you something to add to the content this month.

You can use lots of out and about pictures and selfies, make sure they have a business angle at least half the time, and also promote any networking or meetings with customers you do this month with joint selfies tagging each other and bigging each other up.

May

1	**May Day** Share a memorable experience.	**2**	Out and about, share what you are up to with a selfie.
5	VIDEO – show customers how do you can help them (include CTA).	**6**	Share a testimonial from a customer, tag and celebrate them.
9	GO LIVE – give a top tip.	**10**	Share your latest activity.
13	Share a 'fill in the gap' post, funny if you can.	**14**	Share a testimonial from a customer.
17	Share your latest offers and how people can buy from you.	**18**	Talk about your favourite song, pop a link on if you can.
21	Out and about, share what you are up to with a selfie.	**22**	Flashback day share what were you doing today 5 years ago
25	GO LIVE – talk about your week.	**26**	Share your latest offers (include a CTA).
29	Expert post. Show off your knowledge and build credibility.	**30**	GO LIVE – talk about your latest news.

May was once considered a bad luck month to get married.

May

	GO LIVE – talk about the current market for your business.	**4**	**Star Wars Day** – just go for the silly things!
	Selfie of you a using products.	**8**	Showcase your latest offers (include a CTA).
	Share a selfie of you in a meeting.	**12**	Use a quote related to your business.
	Refer a business colleague and big them up!	**16**	Showcase your products or services, don't use stock images.
	Show customers how you add value to them.	**20**	Ask an engaging question.
	Share your favourite time of day and why.	**24**	Long story post How will your business look like in 2 year's time?
	GO LIVE – talk about what's happening in your field.	**28**	VIDEO – show customers what you do (include CTA).
	Spring Bank Holiday Share a memorable day from this month.		

Military Appreciation Month, Deaf Awareness Week (7th -13th May), World Red Cross Day (8th May).

Your Notes

Specific content ideas for May:

_____

_____

_____

_____

_____

_____

_____

_____

_____

_____

_____

_____

_____

_____

_____

_____

_____

_____

_____

_____

June

June weather continues to be a good content driver, either great weather or bad weather – it works either way! The Summer Solstice happens in the Northern hemisphere in June, so a chance to add that to your ideas and perhaps link the longest days into getting more done or having more time. Festival season also hits us in June so again music and fun can be a massive driver for new content for you.

Father's Day (UK) falls later in June and is often less visual than Mother's Day or Valentine's Day however the content and marketing opportunity is still there. If you don't have a father or man in your life, maybe add content about who has been influential in your life and why. Remember if your product or services DOES relate to Father's Day, try to post as often as you can, don't be afraid you'll cheese people off, you must be visible so post as many times a day, in addition to what's on the planner, if you can.

June

1	VIDEO – show customers your latest news (include CTA).	**2**	Out and about, share what you are up to with a selfie.
5	**World Environment Day** Post something related.	**6**	Share links or resources you use or like.
9	Do a selfie of you with a customer.	**10**	Partner with a business friend and share together.
13	GO LIVE – talk about Father's Day.	**14**	Share your best tips.
17	Share a statistic relating to your business.	**18**	Out and about, share what you are up to with a selfie.
21	**International Day of Yoga** Post something related.	**22**	Long story – talk about a significant male in your life.
25	Showcase your products or services. Don't use stock images.	**26**	Share your latest offers (include CTA).
29	Expert post show off your knowledge and build credibility.	**30**	Share best thing that has happened during this month.

Midsummer's Day falls in the middle of Summer, and is the longest day. Father's Day celebrated.

June

‡ Father's Day visuals.	**4** Expert post – show off your knowledge and build credibility.
ᵍ Father's Day offers or content about me!	**8** Showcase your product or services (include CTA).
1 Put links out to articles or courses you've found useful.	**12** Longer post related to businessmen who have influenced you.
5 VIDEO – explain your business offer (include CTA).	**16** Share a memorable experience with your father or man in your life.
9 Thank a business contact – tag them and big them up!	**20** GO LIVE – talk about latest news in your business.
3 Share a 'fill in the gap' post!	**24** **Midsummer's Day** Share your favourite ice cream.
7 Share a memorable experience (affinity with customers).	**28** VIDEO – show customers what you can offer them.

Great Outdoors Month, Day of the African Child (16ᵗʰ),
Refugee Week (20ᵗʰ - 26ᵗʰ June), Armed Forces Day (25ᵗʰ).

Your Notes

Specific content ideas for June:

_____

_____

_____

_____

_____

_____

_____

_____

_____

_____

_____

_____

_____

_____

_____

_____

_____

_____

_____

_____

July

The big theme for July is summertime and schools breaking up! So lots of new content to drive at even if you chose not to do pictures of your children (which is fine) or don't have any kids, it's a great time to talk about your childhood and add stories about you so your audience get to know you better. Holidays, warm weather, and the work-life balance at this time a year are all something to reflect in your posts to keep things fresh.

It is good to show a different side to you and sharing a little of who you are – people buy from people and so try to make early content that gives your followers an idea of who you feel about important issues.

Please nothing controversial though, you're here to build relationships, not upset people.

July

1 VIDEO – show customers how you can help them (include CTA).		**2** Use a summer quote or meme related to your business.	
5 Long story post about summer for your business.		**6** Share a memorable experience about your school holidays.	
9 Share your happy holiday memories.		**10** Show a Selfie from your holidays.	
13 GO LIVE – talk about your latest business news (include a CTA).		**14** Showcase your products or services with a customer story.	
17 Share a disastrous summer experience.		**18** **World Nelson Mandela Day** Post something related	
21 Long story – talk about favourite holidays past or future!		**22** VIDEO – show offers, products or services (include CTA)	
25 VIDEO – show customers how you celebrate Summer.		**26** Showcase your product or service.	
29 Product or service visuals include a how to buy link.		**30** GO LIVE – talk about what have you be up to in your business	

July is the month dedicated to freedom, independen and celebrations of country and culture.

July

3 GO LIVE – talk about your business promos (include CTA).	**4** **Independence Day (USA)** Post something related.
Share summer offers or deals.	**8** GO LIVE – talk about what happening in your business (include CTA).
1 VIDEO – show customers what your business can offer them.	**12** Give a testimonial to someone else.
5 Out and about, share what you are up to with a selfie.	**16** Share a thought provoking 'fill in the gap' post.
9 Share links you find helpful, and tag a potential customer.	**20** GO LIVE – talk about your business challenges or struggles.
3 Set up a a poll related to your business.	**24** Share a behind the scenes picture or story.
7 Long post – how you feel when you help a customer.	**28** Show a testimonial and why you're so proud of it.
Share best moment from this month.	

Plastic Free Month, National Transplant Week (7th- 14th), World Population Day (11th), Carousel Day (25th).

Your Notes

Specific content ideas for July:

_____

_____

_____

_____

_____

_____

_____

_____

_____

_____

_____

_____

_____

_____

_____

_____

_____

_____

_____

_____

August

The summer theme and holiday content continue this month with some opportunities to show the non-working side of you. YES, you need to keep posting on ALL platforms whilst you are on holiday, it's 10 minutes a day every day, and as you know visibility is key so either schedule content or just do it first thing in the day so it's done!

It's about making relationships, and this is a real opportunity for you to network and build loyal followers. 'Early bird' offers can help you secure sales in what can be a quieter time of the year and help you market to your network.

August

1	Share your favourite emoji.	**2**	GO LIVE – talk about business successes (include CTA).
5	Expert post. Show off your knowledge and build credibility.	**6**	Share your latest news.
9	Use a quote related to your business.	**10**	Out and about, share what you are up to with a selfie.
13	Add a link to a favourite music group or song, tell a story about it.	**14**	Showcase how your services or products help people.
17	Have a flashback day, last week, month, or year.	**18**	Use a quote related to your business.
21	Share a testimonial from a customer.	**22**	Share a memorable holiday experience.
25	GO LIVE – talk about your latest offers and products.	**26**	Thank a customer, friend, or business contact and tag them.
29	Take pictures of your products or services and showcase them.	**30**	Expert post show off your knowledge.

August is a month of Summer vacation and holidays.

August

Selfie of you, using your products or delivering your services.	4	Showcase your latest offers and how you help others.
Make a joke about the weather.	8	VIDEO – show customers your offers (include CTA).
Share a summer 'fill in the gap' post.	1 2	**International Youth Day** Show a youthful you!
Long story post about your plans for the rest of the year.	1 6	Recommend a book for Summer reading.
GO LIVE – talk about your lifestyle and what you love to do.	20	Share your latest offers and how people can connect with you.
Advance promotion of Bank Holiday offers.	24	GO LIVE – talk about your customers and who they are.
Share your latest successes and wins.	28	Share a hobby that you regularly do.
VIDEO – show customers how you add value.		

Happiness Happens Month, World Wide Web Day (1st), Blogger Day (5th), International Left Handers Day (13th).

Your Notes

Specific content ideas for August:

_____

_____

_____

_____

_____

_____

_____

_____

_____

_____

_____

_____

_____

_____

_____

_____

_____

_____

_____

_____

September

Lots of opportunities for September themes and content, have you considered an end of Summer Sale for your products or services? You don't have to discount, consider offering bundles rather than selling a single item or service. This can be a great way to get more income for the same amount of marketing and business time. Think about *'buy one, get one-half price'*, or *'30 minutes extra when you book 60 minutes'*, that sort of thing. Be creative and tempt people that have been lurking (*remember the 'lurkers'*) all summer to purchase from you now. Plus, this can get a much-needed income after what can be an expensive time of year.

Other content drivers can be back to school offers or stories, if you don't have children, then reflect on your schooling or educational experiences and let others know more about you. You can make some great posts about early days, school life, friends you had and early careers to that can all link beautifully into why you do what you do now!

September

1 Product or service visuals, remind people what it is you do.		**2** GO LIVE - talk about what's next now the holiday season is over.	
5 Share your latest offers or special deals.		**6** Share a memorable experience about your school days.	
9 Discuss a statistic relating to your business and why it's important.		**10** **World Suicide Prevention Day** Post something related.	
13 GO LIVE - talk about your business and what you're up to.		**14** Put links out to articles you have written or like.	
17 Out and about, share what you are up to with a selfie.		**18** VIDEO - show customers how you help them (include CTA).	
21 **International Day of Peace** Post something related.		**22** Showcase your latest offers, deals or promotions.	
25 Out and about, share what you are up to with a selfie.		**26** Have a flashback day to last year.	
29 Share a favourite app. you use in your business.		**30** Share what has been your highlight from this month.	

The first month of Autumn (Fall). The Time for Harvest and Harvest Festivals.

September

Share your Back to School messages and thoughts.	**4**	Selfie of you at work or using products.
VIDEO – show customers your offers, products or services (include CTA).	**8**	Give a business tip away!
Share how this book has help you with your social media.	**12**	GO LIVE – talk about your latest business news (include a CTA).
Share a 'fill in the gap' post or funny meme.	**16**	Long story post about your business at this time of year.
Give a referral to someone and tag them in.	**20**	Selfie of you at work and why you love what you do.
GO LIVE – talk about your business and offer expert advice.	**24**	Showcase your product or service and how people can connect.
Share a testimonial from a customer.	**28**	Share a story using a business or family photo around education.

Friendship Month, Read a Book Month, Boss/Employee Exchange Day (14th), Business Woman Day (22nd).

Your Notes

Specific content ideas for September:

_____

_____

_____

_____

_____

_____

_____

_____

_____

_____

_____

_____

_____

_____

_____

_____

_____

_____

_____

_____

October

October's biggest theme should be to prepare for Christmas! Yes, this early! Set the seed now and share posts and content about what your products or services have to offer around the Christmas season... Yes, the links may be HUGE, or they can be tenuous, but Christmas is THE sales opportunity of the year, especially if you get in early, so don't be shy. If you REALLY can't link in any way, maybe theme your content around others in your network and ask them what offers they have or tag them with their posts. Be generous with your content and help others to do well.

Other ideas can be around darker evenings, donating to food banks or school Harvest Festivals or charity work you could link in with and share. Diwali, the Hindu Festival of Light, also celebrated by people of Jain and Sikh faiths so again this connection with other communities shows you are open to working with anyone and have acceptance and respect for all faiths. Check which date this falls on as it changes every year.

Halloween is always on 31st and can be another fun theme or sales opportunity, don't forget to have lots of interesting images in your content.

October

1	GO LIVE – talk about what you're up to this month.	**2**	Share your latest offers, show off Christmas deals.
5	Showcase your services or products tag your best customers.	**6**	Ask an engaging question about the darker nights
9	Share a memorable experience and why it's important to you.	**10**	**World Mental Health Day** Post something related.
13	Long story post about why you love your work.	**14**	Share latest news relating to your business.
17	VIDEO – show customers how you can help them.	**18**	Share an offer for Halloween or Christmas.
21	Show customers how you add value to them, tag new customers.	**22**	GO LIVE – talk about the customers you've met this week.
25	Share a memorable experience from your previous work life.	**26**	Showcase your services or products include to buy from yc
29	Product or service visuals – include a spooky theme if possible.	**30**	VIDEO – show customers what you d dress up Halloween sty

Hindu festival of lights, Diwali. Yom Kippur and Sukkot sometimes fall this month. Clocks go BACK

October

3	Out and about, share what you are up to with a selfie.	**4**	Share links to another business.
7	GO LIVE – talk about your plans for Halloween or Christmas.	**8**	VIDEO – show customers products or services and what you do for them.
11	Share a Halloween or Christmas 'fill in the gap' post.	**12**	Use an inspirational quote related to your business.
15	Start a Countdown to your latest offer or special deal.	**16**	Long story post about you and your business successes.
19	Have a flashback day, explain why you have posted it.	**20**	Product or service visuals – include a spooky or Christmas theme.
23	Have a flashback day – what were you doing a year or 5 years ago?	**24**	Share a statistic relating to your business at this time of year.
27	GO LIVE – talk about your business and link to this month's theme.	**28**	Share your latest news or ideas.
31	**Halloween** Post something related.		

Fire Prevention Month, National Curry Week, World Smile Day (2nd), World Online Networking Day (29th).

Your Notes

Specific content ideas for October:

_____

_____

_____

_____

_____

_____

_____

_____

_____

_____

_____

_____

_____

_____

_____

_____

_____

_____

_____

_____

November

If it's relevant to you, the main focus could be promoting Christmas offers, services and products. Be confident that people struggle for new ideas, and are pleased if you can give them a solution to a gift or activity they like. Make it very easy for them to buy.

Remembrance Day (11th) is a big theme for November and in the USA it can link to the Thanksgiving celebrations. It's important to show respect and reflection around wider world events.

Hanukkah is a Jewish Festival and like Diwali is a Festival of Light. It's useful to mention these themes in your content. Remember to check specific dates each year. Guy Fawkes Night (5th Nov in UK) and *'Bonfire or Fireworks'* events can have fun images and themes.

Later in the month, usually on the last Friday, it's Black Friday sales and promotion opportunities again, so hit these massively if you can as the *'shopping for Christmas'* gathers momentum. Remember to make your offer clear, state your process, and make it very easy for the customer to contact you and buy from you.

November

1	VIDEO – show customers how you add value and your current offers.	**2**	Use a quote or Meme related to your business.
5	**Guy Fawkes Night (UK)** Post something related.	**6**	Post a testimonial about someone.
9	Promote Black Friday offers or share others.	**10**	Give a follower a 'Shout Out'.
13	**World Kindness Day** What act of kindness can your business give?	**14**	Expert post to show off your knowledge/credibility.
17	Use a quote or meme related to your business.	**18**	GO LIVE – talk about your business in the run-up to Christmas
21	Put links out to websites you use and enjoy.	**22**	Out and about, share what you are up to with a selfie.
25	VIDEO – show customers how you serve them (include CTA).	**26**	Post Black Friday visuals or tags.
29	Share something you have purchased and never use and why.	**30**	Share your biggest learning moment this month.

Thanksgiving Day (USA) falls on 4th Thursday in November followed by Black Friday the next day.

November

Long story post about how you feel at this time of year.	**4** GO LIVE – talk about your Black Friday offers early.
Long story post about how you feel at this time of year.	**8** Share a buying experience about 'bargains' you've seen.
Black Friday visuals, your products, or what you want to buy and why!	**12** Share a testimonial from a customer, make sure it's everywhere!
Ask a themed and engaging question.	**16** Promote Black Friday offers and how people can buy from you.
Share a 'fill in the gap' post!	**20** Showcase your services or products (include a CTA).
Share a link to your customer's product or service.	**24** Expert post – show off your knowledge and build credibility.
Post a funny Meme.	**28** Flashback day, what were you doing this time last year?

Adoption Month, Stress Awareness Day (4th), Tongue Twister Day (8th), International Men's Day (19th).

Your Notes

Specific content ideas for November:

_____

_____

_____

_____

_____

_____

_____

_____

_____

_____

_____

_____

_____

_____

_____

_____

_____

_____

_____

_____

_____

December

I f you sell a product or service that has ANY link to the festive season, then in this month EVERY POST must be around that offer; how it helps people, how you love it and how people can buy it.

Every post must directly or indirectly link to Christmas. Visibility is key and social media is so busy this time of year that posts only show in people's newsfeed for seconds. *Don't feel nervous – get it out there and make money.*

The Advent period can offer a lovely theme of content, Day 1, Day 2, etc (or even the 12 days of Christmas song!) so if you have lots of different products or services you could prepare some great visuals and use them daily in content. The weather, the longest day, and Winter Solstice plus people feeling stressed can also be great content drivers – remember to keep it upbeat and empathetic.

YES, you need to have content prepared over Christmas, especially if you're doing a Boxing Day or January Sale launch which are always popular on social media as people are usually bored and scrolling through their phones after just a day. Family time images, holiday fun, or even disasters are great to share if you're happy to. New Year's Eve celebrations need sharing with care but are always good fun and lets you tag customers, followers, and friends.

December

1	VIDEO – show customers Christmas offers you have.	**2**	Expert post to show off your knowledge/credibility.
5	Share a memorable Christmas experience.	**6**	Product or service visuals and how to buy now for Christmas.
9	Share a 'fill in the gap' post – Christmas themed of course!	**10**	Give your favourite Christmas family Tradition.
13	Share a memorable experience about your Festive season.	**14**	Share a customer's testimonial and share their offers too.
17	Ask an engagement question, what makes an ideal Christmas for you?	**18**	Out and about, share what you are up to with a Christmas selfie
21	GO LIVE – talk about your business and why you are proud of it.	**22**	Use a Christmas quote related to your business.
25	**Christmas Day** Post something related.	**26**	**Boxing Day (UK)** Post something related.
29	Ask an engagement question or post a silly meme for New Year.	**30**	Give a MASSIVE thank you to all your customers.

Happy Christmas and a Prosperous New Year!

December

GO LIVE - talk about your business at this time of year.	**4** Share Christmas offers and experiences.
Long story post about your business at Christmas.	**8** GO LIVE – talk about your business during this season (include CTA).
VIDEO – show customers what you can offer them now and in the future.	**12** Selfie time, you out shopping or enjoying a school play, etc.
Showcase your products or services, themed if possible (include CTA).	**16** Post the deadline for your Christmas offers.
GO LIVE – talk about your latest business news and offers.	**20** Christmas offers, show what you've purchased, tag small businesses.
Silly Christmas memes or photos of you past or present.	**24** **Christmas Eve** Share some Christmas Eve pictures.
Share a 'Betwixtmas' update, are you working or resting?	**28** Showcase your product or services with a 'January Sale' theme.
New Year Eve How will you celebrate the arrival of New Year?	

Write a Business Plan Month, Disability Day (3rd), Human Rights Day (10th), Day of Reconciliation (16th).

Your Notes

Specific content ideas for December:

_____

_____

_____

_____

_____

_____

_____

_____

_____

_____

_____

_____

_____

_____

_____

_____

_____

_____

_____

_____

_____

_____

Part 5
Maximum Results
in Minimal Time

*All we have to decide is
what to do with the time
that is given us.*

J R R Tolkien

Use Your Time Wisely

A s you know the purpose of this book is to allow you to have a daily social media presence for your business on any platform in 10 minutes a day. Obviously the more you put in, the more you get out in terms of connecting with the right people, showing off your business, building relationships, and just *'getting out there'*. A daily to-do list should look something like this:

Action	Time	Done
Post your chosen content from the planner on your specific platform.	2 minutes	
Check notifications and respond to as many as you can in the allotted time.	3 minutes	
Like 5 posts from your followers (different ones every day).	1 minute	
Comment on 5 posts from your followers (different ones to the posts above).	2 minutes	
Add new contacts – think about your ideal customer and add 20 every day on each platform.	2 minutes	

If you can do this more than once a day, then that's even better but consistency is the key. This is the BUSINESS time you have on your chosen social media and so multiply it if you have more than one platform you are using. Should you just *'pop'* onto social media for your fun, then try to connect with your ideal customers. Avoid consuming social media if you can, your job is to put content out there, not read others too much!

> *Whether you think you can,*
> *or think you can't – you're right.*
>
> Henry Ford

Using a Scheduling Tool

Scheduling can ease the pressure for you and allow you to do all the basic daily posts and content scheduling in one hit. *I do mine once a week.* This means you can have more time to respond to comments and perhaps post additional ad-hoc things as inspiration strikes.

It's also really useful for marketing for events or specific promotions such as Mother's Day or Summer Sales.

I suggest you try one of the following as they ALL offer free packages, which are useful as they allow you to learn if scheduling in advance works for you and your business. It allows you to find out which platform you feel works easiest for you and then, if you find that advanced scheduling is convenient for you, maybe you can invest in upgrading to a paid package - the choice is yours!

> *The first rule of any technology used in a business is that automation applied to an efficient operation will magnify the efficiency. The second is that automation applied to an inefficient operation will magnify the inefficiency.*
>
> Bill Gates

A Quick Overview of FREE Scheduling Sites

Buffer - they have a free plan which works with Facebook, Twitter, LinkedIn, and Instagram. It allows you three social media accounts on the free plan and max's out at 30 posts in 30 days. It has a basic report which tells you which posts are popular and unpopular which is useful and has a scheduling planner which allows you to *'drag and drop'* posts where you need them.

Crowdfire - this is a social media management app that helps you discover and schedule content and manage your social accounts in one place. The free plan offers scheduling on the usual 4 platforms. The free offer is quite limited but does allow you to try it out and claims to offer better value packages once you upgrade than the other competitors.

Facebook - good old FB lets you schedule content using its app if you have a group or a page, and this is totally free, so this is an easy win if its your platform of choice?

Hootsuite - this also works on the same 4 platforms and offers a similar free set up with 3 social media accounts and 30 posts per month. It has an easy to use scheduling calendar and some simple reporting to guide you. There is an online library for images too. The online *'training academy'* to help new users is simple and quickly gets you started.

Later - this is a visual platform and unlike some of the others allows Pinterest on it as well as Facebook and Twitter. Its main users are from Instagram. The free plan is with one social account per platform, one user, 30 Instagram posts, 50 Twitter posts, 30 Facebook posts, and 30 Pinterest posts per month. Basic analytics are also available.

Socialoomph - this platform's free plan is different as it only applies to one social media platform at no cost but it does allow you to schedule posts (maximum 3 per hour) on one social media profile. So, if you are concentrating all of your efforts on just one platform, this could be a real winner for you. The initial set up is reported as being tricky, but once it's done it's a basic and practical interface.

Free trials too!

There are LOTS of other social media planning platforms and many offer free trials too, so do give them a go. I use one and find that a binge once a week for an hour or so gives me time to plan the more strategic posts and frees up my time elsewhere for the fun connecting stuff, safe in the knowledge I'm always *'out there'*. Remember to link up with me on your platform of choice.

Pricing

Once you have tried a few different tools, the best for your business needs will soon become clear. If you choose to invest be very careful about the return on investment. Some scheduling platforms are great value at £20 per month, others can be £99 or more per month so do look into this carefully. *I feel that starting with a free plan and working with this for a while will show if the investment is really worth it and then go with what works for you.*

In-depth analytics might be interesting, but will you use them? Thirty-five different social media platforms sound great, but why do you need to be on so many?

Do not rush in but remember to leverage your time with social media too, £20 a month is a takeaway coffee in London once a week. For that small investment, you could be less stressed and more visible. *That sounds like a great return on investment to me.*

Your Notes

How can I make scheduling work for me?

_____

_____

_____

_____

_____

_____

_____

_____

---

*However difficult life may seem,
there is always something
you can do and succeed at.*

Stephen Hawking

Part 6
Marketing Basics

Always deliver more than expected.

Larry Page
Co-founder of Google

Sell Without Selling

Y ou might hear the term *'sell without selling'* when you are using social media as a marketing tool. Sales and marketing can often be seen as a specialist task and one which many small businesses fail to focus on, often to their detriment.

This book focuses on connecting and being visible to potential customers every day, sharing your business with them and building relationships. If they don't want to buy from you now, that's fine, they might buy later or recommend you to someone they know.

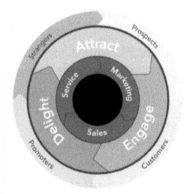

Remember the image of The Flywheel Effect at the beginning of the book?

Every day you are working on building an online presence that helps you connect with people in the first place, then to focus on the people out there on your chosen platform who match your ideal customer profile.

| 121

Strangers - if your profile is an open one (recommended) your content can be seen by strangers and they are ALL potential customers in the very busy world of social media and will often just connect on an ad-hoc basis.

Prospects - these are people who have not yet bought from you, or even made contact with any of your comments or posts but are 'lurkers' and could just be keeping an eye on you and enjoying your views on life or having a *'nose around'* your business.

Customers - followers that have bought from you before and might do so again, so it's important to stay connected to them and keep them interested in your content.

Promoters - followers who love what you do and will share your content and regularly engage and support you. These can be nurtured and are important to you.

Your work here is to use the planner content, along with your *'spin'* to attract, engage, and delight your followers. This can sometimes be called a 'marketing funnel' and so the top layer is strangers, then further down the funnel, they become prospects.

After this, if you continue to nurture them, they will usually become customers then promoters, all working their way down your sales funnel to becoming regular customers. If you offer them a great experience and look after them, many customers can become great promoters and you can help each other out by sharing content and tagging each other's material, to the benefit of both of you!

When you have connected with these people, you have moved from the grey outside ring to the next ring in the flywheel, a step closer to 'sell without selling'. Your content and consistency will ensure you are driving people into the sales funnel in the next circle using the three key concepts of attracting, engaging, and delighting.

If people like you, they'll listen to you,
but if they trust you,
they'll do business with you.

Zig Ziglar

Attract - many of the posts from the planner involve highly visual content, as research shows this is the most effective way of attracting people to your content. Try to use clear and interesting photos, memes, videos, and images that are original to you and your business. By placing a different type of post daily and using a theme to follow from the planners means there is a constant source of original content to attract people to you and what you can offer.

Engage - lots of your posts offer an opportunity to your followers to comment or respond, this engagement is very important, so always check your notifications and respond if you can. Use humour if you can, we all need some fun and sometimes social media can be a *'dark place'* so keep your content light and positive as much as you possibly can. Always try to comment on others' posts too, even just a like or thumbs up shows you're out there and building relationships.

Delight - sharing personal viewpoints or stories about you and your business offer(s) a more intimate insight to you and what you do, this is something that delights potential customers as they want to buy from someone they know, like and trust.

Give them a WOW every time they see your content, let them know how you can help them and be of service to them. Make it a delight to do business with you and follow you on Facebook or your preferred platform; this helps turn customers into promoters.

Sales, Service and Marketing

The central part is more specific content about what you do and how people can buy products or services from you, the hardest marketing part and only a small percentage of content on the planner has a CTA directing customers to buy here, buy this, or click here to find out more.

Sell without selling is about being transparent with your offer and pricing, being clear about how people can buy from you, and offering them your expert guidance and advice for free whenever you can.

The planner has a balance of content posts to allow you to do this without being pushy or too focused on what YOU want from the connection, not what they want from it. The content of the planner is designed to be 'evergreen' so that you invest once and use it forever.

This does mean that some of the dates and events that change yearly need YOU to plan in the dates and possible actions on the planner to make sure you never miss an opportunity to *sell without selling* ' plus, each business and its audience are different.

Christmas is a MASSIVE opportunity if you are selling gift products, but perhaps less so if you are a fitness guru where January requires your focus. *It's important to know your business, its best selling months and your ideal customer.*

I have given you some ideas on how to market your product or service in a way that maximises your sales potential, shows you off to your audience, and generates more income and engagement. You may have some questions:

How far in advance do I start marketing for an event?

I'd say 4 weeks is the minimum, 6 weeks ideal, as people will be scrolling through their social media for ideas, bargains and offers that match their own needs and are easy to buy. If you are 'first out there' with a great marketing campaign, and keep it up during the entire period, you're on to a winner.

Do I post content from the planner plus special offers?

Ideally, YES! You need to stick to the planner if you can, to get a balance of content but then post additional content whenever you can specifically around your offer. It can be the offer itself, visuals, videos, lives – follow the planner but around the service or product you are promoting.

If you are selling different things you need to use different posts. This may feel pushy or that you are doing TOO much but you are not. You need to be visible in your world, to engage and promote your offer. *Please don't be shy - go for it.* You know by now the life of a social media post varies from platform to platform but often the newsfeed is so fast-paced, and certainly at busy times of the year, such as Christmas, that you need to *'up your game'* and get sales content out there more than you would normally do.

Make it easy to buy!

Creating a way that makes it very simple and easy for your customers to buy is a sure-fire winner to marketing success – if people are scrolling and click on your product, they will probably *'pass you by'* unless there is an easy way to find out more about it and buy – preferably online.

Consider using linked products like Landing Pages, PayPal, or Instant Messenger which are all worth the effort to add to your posts. It means maximising the *'impulse'* buy and the *'I want it now'* mindset of many social media users.

There is various online *'click to pay'* services, from PayPal through to Stripe. Nearly all of them take a commission so you have to decide whether or not you want to have these on your platform to make buying easy and to plan how you will respond to online-only sales to ensure your customer is always delighted with the product you've sold or the service they have purchased. Online platforms, such as Etsy, are also really useful to look into for easy selling.

Creating offers

Using the monthly planners gives you ideas on what's coming up and when. You can use the themes or events that link into your type of business or if there is no fit, you can create your offer with the different ideas every month on the planner. These are touched on briefly in the planner and here are some more marketing ideas you can use to suit your individual needs and the type of business you run.

The 6 P's of Marketing

The original *'4 P's' of Marketing*, by Shapiro in the 1980s, is referred to as *'The Marketing Mix'*. The P's being Product, Price, Promotion, and Placement - the key things you need to focus on for success. Like most theories, this has been adapted over time and now, as the image shows, has the additions of Process and People. Let me explain this further:

PRODUCT (or SERVICE) - all of your content is aimed at showing off what you offer customers and potential customers who buy with you. If it's a service, be very clear on what you do to help them how you add value and why you're the best person for them to use for this specific area. If it's a product, again sell the benefits, go into detail if appropriate, and use lots of images to help you show off the item you are selling.

If you offer lots of different things make your content clear and simple. Sell one thing at a time to one person, don't *'spray and pray'* your different products and services around, it confuses your followers and dilutes your message.

PRICE - I always believe you should be as transparent with your pricing as possible. *Not everyone agrees with me on this.* Often your offer is bespoke so never mislead your audience with a price that appears low and then turns out to be significantly different. For some businesses it's around explaining the value of your offer prior to sharing specific prices, for others being up front on how people buy from you is a breath of fresh air.

Do some research on your product or services then add an hourly or daily 'salary' to it, ensuring you don't work for a pittance. *Remember, you're in business to make money.* Don't be afraid to be more expensive than your competition, you can prove that what you do is better or different than them in your marketing and it is ALWAYS easier to drop a price by offering a discount or promotion, rather than trying to increase a price at a later date.

PROMOTION - There are lots of different types of promotions out there, January or Black Friday sales are classic promotional opportunities and are covered in the planner but there are other ideas you might want to play with if you fancy trying something new?

BOGOF - Buy one, get one free - a simple offer and useful for high margin products or services or if you need to clear out older stock. Only use as a short term offer as they can be hard on profit margins and you need to maintain your income. A nice way to promote once and get two sales from something you would otherwise have hanging around taking up space and holding equity. Be careful not to offer BOGOF's to just regular customers who would buy anyway, but use also to attract new people to your business.

BOGOHP - Buy one, get one half price - as with the BOGOF but less impactful on your margins and useful on higher-priced services. Ensure you include any additional delivery costs or charges in your offer details. **WIGIG – when it's gone, it's gone** - having a clear out, running a special deal or wanting to generate short term interest in a specific service or produce, the WIGIG acronym should be used sparingly and in a targeted manner. If you put people under pressure to buy, for them to see 6 weeks later there was no need, they'll feel cheated.

Countdown to Buy - really good if you're selling at a discount until a certain time or looking to attract people that are wavering on a purchase. The countdown to buy approach is good at generating last minute sales. These can be genuine issues, such as posting times for Christmas (which you MUST get right or face the social media backlash) or create your own deadlines. Often a Sunday evening as a deadline to buy works best, think of buying from eBay, how many things do you follow with an offer, only to find that you're pipped to the post 5 minutes before it closes on a Sunday night. *Classic marketing!*

PLACE - originally this was about the location your product was on the supermarket shelf, or the location of your office, but times move on and the place in the virtual world refers to the social media platform you market your business on.

This links back to the research and heavy thinking you did at the beginning of the book – which social media platform is the best in order to meet your ideal customer and promote your business to them. If you are doing ALL of the right things in the wrong place, then no one will see them. If you think this might be an issue for you, turn back a few chapters and make sure your 10 minutes a day is spent in the right 'place' for you to succeed.

PROCESSES - this has already been touched on and is around how does the customer find out more or buy from you. It's really important that a potential customer can connect with you and buy from you easily and quickly. The world of social media has no patience and if you make it hard for them to get what they want, they'll simply go elsewhere. Links to web pages or endless forms can be really off-putting, so give a lot of thought to the buying process and make it simple, quick and easy to use on a mobile phone as the majority of social media buying is from a mobile device rather than a PC or laptop.

I never dreamed about success,
I worked for it.

Estee Lauder

PEOPLE - I have repeatedly said, *'sell without selling'* as social media is about relationship building and *'people buy from people'*, refers to those they know, like or trust even more so. The planner has a range of different posts and encourages you to share certain personal content. I often get feedback that people don't want to *'sell their personal life'* online, and I understand that so don't cross any boundaries you have and don't move away from your principles. Make the stories and memories you share happy ones, but non-specific.

👍 Only post family selfies or pictures of your home if you want to. Don't feel the need to put photos of your partner or children online if this feels wrong or uncomfortable to you.

👍 It's important to share your business persona, your experience, expertise, and knowledge with potential customers with honesty and integrity.

👍 A timely reminder is people buy from people, not stock images, Memes or GIFs.

Part 7
Glossary,
References and
Acknowledgements

Marketing is no longer about the stuff that you make, but about the stories you tell.

Seth Godin

Glossary

Word	Description
Affinity	Liking someone or something. Feeling like you are in the same spot with someone and they 'get' you.
Algorithm	The underpinning programme of the social media platform (that changes frequently) and dictates wh ich posts get seen and how.
Call to Action (CTA)	When you ask the reader to take an action having read your post - so follow this link, click here, call to book, that sort of thing.
Engage/ engagement	If people actively comments or 'like' a post, they are seen to have engaged with it - this is what you are looking for.
Flatlay	A staged prepared background, placed on a flat surface, used to show off your products in a stylish and attractive manner.
Flywheel Effect	A concept developed by Jim Collins: converting an audience to paying customers.
Follows	The number of different people that actively follow you on social media.
Hashtag #	A method of linking your post with a group of similar posts - to be searched easily.
Ideal Customer	Marketing term to identify and describe your one perfect customer, helps to target your marketing to the right people.
Incremental Change	A change in a process, person or situation that happens in small steps over time.

Word	Description
LIVE	Video done 'live' on your chosen platform, not pre-recorded and uploaded, allows for audience interaction.
Lurkers	A term for people that follow you but never engage or comment on your posts.
Meme	A pre-prepared image or message you can use to post with, can be funny, thoughtful or market specific.
Platform	The chosen social media platform you use to promote your business.
Sales Funnel (see Flywheel Effect)	Another marketing concept to explain converting a larger audience to paying customers buy getting them to move through a virtual funnel.
Scrollers	People who spend a lot of time on social media platforms without real purpose.
SMART Goals	An acronym which helps set firm targets. It means Specific, Measurable, Achievable, Relevant and Time-bound.
SME	Small to Medium sized Business - a smaller company with between 5 - 50 employees.
Socials	The slang word for chosen social media platform you use to promote your business.
Sole Trader	Someone who is self employed and works alone.
Tagging @	When you purposefully add an individual to a post by using their name in order to ensure they see your post.
The Marketing Mix	A concept developed by Benson P. Shapiro in the 1980's to help business focus on their marketing activity.
Views	The number of people who see your post.

References

Welcome to the Social Media Jungle!

Website

Digital Natives, Digital Immigrants. On the Horizon, M Prensky, (MCB University Press, Vol. 9 No. 5, October 2001) https://www.google.com/search?customer=firefox-b-d&q=digital+native+prensky, 09/09/20

Marketing 101: Flywheel vs Funnel, Brooklin Nash, (Trust Radius), https://www.trustradius.com/buyer-blog/marketing-flywheel-vs-funnel, 29/10/20

Flywheel, Jim Collins.com, Jim Collins, (Jim Collins) https://www.jimcollins.com/concepts/the-flywheel.html

Part 1: Creating a Habit

Collins James, C, Good to Great: Why Some Companies Make the Leap... (Random House Business) 2001

Website

Creating a Business Social Media Habit, Habit Guide, JamesClear.com, J Clear (James Clear) https://jamesclear.com/habit-guide, 09/09/20

Part 2: Which Social Media Platforms are Right for my Business?

Website

Facebook Statistics: https://www.facebook.com/business/marketing/facebook

Which platforms to use, Statistics & data, Omnicore Agency, Editorial Team, (Omnicore Group) www.omnicoreagency.com, 09/09/20

Part 4: Quick Success Monthly Planner

Website

Planners, Easter & Ramadan, Insider.Com, Editorial Team, (Insider Inc) Insider.com/how-april-fools-day-is-celebrated-in-11-countries-around-the-world-2017-3, 09/09/20

Days of the Year, Brandon Withey, (Days of the Year) https://www.daysoftheyear.com, 08/10/20

Part 6: Marketing Basics

Shapiro, Benson P, Concept of the Marketing Mix, (Harvard Business School) 1981

Website

Flywheel, Jim Collins.com, Jim Collins, (Jim Collins) https://www.jimcollins.com/concepts/the-flywheel.html

Image

Marketing 101: Flywheel vs Funnel, Brooklin Nash, (Trust Radius), https://www.trustradius.com/buyer-blog/marketing-flywheel-vs-funnel, 29/10/20

Acknowledgements

I would like to express my gratitude to the special people who have helped me produce this book and give me the support and inspiration to complete it, especially in what has, and continues to be a challenging year for everyone across the world.

Firstly, to the most important person in my life, Eric Burton, my wonderful son who has put up with his mum stuck to either her laptop, in a Zoom call or on her phone. He is the most brilliant star in the sky and gives me more than he will ever know, as only a mother can understand.

This moves me on to my own, adorable crazy mother, taken away from me far too early and who was herself a published author of several books. I always admired her for this achievement and was proud to show off her books to whomever I could entice onto the subject. She would be so thrilled to know I've somehow managed to publish my own book and it's a bittersweet experience having to do this without her.

I'd like to mention the fantastic author, Carole Gaskell and her book *Your Pocket Life Coach: 10 minutes a Day to Transforms your Life and Work*. I purchased this book way back in the early 00's and it was my first introduction to the power of coaching and incremental change, which has formed the basis of this book and indeed my career. Her simple and warm message of change alongside an assurance that such change was possible was incredibly powerful for me at the time, literally life changing, and it's a book I still pick up and use to this day.

To my many clients and business friends who have been my teachers along the way, who have put their trust in my ability to lead, inspire and motivate them to change – without them I would not have the knowledge and experience I share with you in this book.

And, of course, my many friends outside of business who are my mates, chums and cheerleaders on every new challenge I face, from running marathons to writing this book. I'm lucky to have you and love you all.

Finally, but not least, my amazing Publisher, Ladey who, along with her daughter, Abbirose at Ladey Adey Publications who have had the patience of saints, the insight of experience and the eye to detail I have never possessed; without them this book would have remained on the bucket list rather than a reality. Just fantastic.

Part 8
About the Author

You are never too small
to make a difference.

Greta Thunberg
(Environmental Activist)

About the Author

Cath Babbington has managed, lectured, trained and taught in many different organisations in her 30+ year career in business. Cath says: *"As CoachCathUK, my focus has been dedicated to growing the coaching practice in all sorts of organisations, as I find I enjoy this more and more."*

Cath has enjoyed working with a string of high flying customers over the years across many different industries from retail to logistics to manufacturing and leisure. She has an ever-growing profile including a regular appearance on Radio Newark about business and a feature in the book *Successful Business Networking Online* by Ladey Adey.

Alongside her work of supporting businesses locally and across the UK, Cath also lectures at various academic institutions in all areas of Business Management and Human Resource Management.

A working mum, a keen, if slow, runner and all-round busy person, Cath's passion is to provide, pragmatic, simple and effective solutions that can be used by everyone to help them be successful in business.

Cath says, *"This first book is the first of many around the 10 minutes a day ethos, based on my experience and results over decades of success and I can't wait to start the next one!"*

Cath can be contacted:

Website: https://www.coachcathuk.com

Facebook: https://www.facebook.com/coachcathuk

Instagram: https://www.instagram.com/coachcathuk/

LinkedIn: https://www.linkedin.com/in/cathie-babbington-coach-teacher-expert-89b3b717/

Index

10 minutes a day with Coach Cath - Business Social Media

The way you treat your
users or customers,
and how you personally
present yourself through
social media, is a way to
differentiate yourself
from your competitors.

Alexis Ohanian, Reddit Co-Founder

146